'I'D LIKE TO BE THE
QUEEN OF PEOPLE'S
HEARTS.'

DIANA

STYLE ICON

DAN JONES

Illustrated by Fernando Monroy

Hardie Grant

BOOKS

INTRODUCTION

Diana Spencer (1961–1997), the young, shy, and famously doe-eyed British noble, became an object of obsession for the international tabloid press following her engagement and marriage to Charles, Prince of Wales. Navigating fandom previously unknown in the pre-social media age, Diana emerged as an icon of style, ripping up and re-writing the royal playbook, right up until her untimely death in 1997.

There are endless reportage photographs of the princess walking the red carpet, glittering in couture, or striding across city streets in oversized collegiate sweats, a baseball cap tugged down over her hair, post-workout. Images of her flood Instagram, reminding us of her enduring significance, intrigue and our fever-pitch fascination with the late, great royal. Celebrities and influencers continue to draw inspiration from her – Virgil Abloh dedicated an entire Off-White show to her, Rihanna cites her as a style influence, and both Frank Ocean and Lena Dunham have paid homage to her. For Netflix's *The Crown*, award-winning costume designer Amy Roberts went one step further, eloquently recreating Diana's most memorable looks for British actress Emma Corrin.

Like so many of us, the teenage Diana Spencer was wonderfully uncool. She wore cutesy ruffled shirts with ribbon ties, loose-fit sweaters with straight skirts or jeans; she was painfully shy, and failed her school exams – twice. The daughter of the 8th Earl Spencer and Frances Shand Kydd eked out a meandering career as a part-time cook, nanny, and taught at an exclusive kindergarten – but then she was reintroduced to Charles (she first met him aged 16, when he briefly courted her sister) and the palace. Thrust into the spotlight, Diana was forced to makeover her look, pose and prospects, transforming almost overnight with a freshly minted romantic, regal edge.

As Charles's fiancée, the princess' fan base was immense. Posh Diana wannabes who lived near London's exclusive Sloane Square earned themselves the nickname 'Sloane ranger' and were lampooned in Ann Barr and Peter York's tongue-in-cheek book *The Official Sloane Ranger Handbook*. To Barr and York, the young princess was the ultimate 1980s super-Sloane. As they noted, 'and the lush taffeta rustle of big skirts after eight... and granny's multi-strand pearl choker.'

'We were told when we got engaged that the media would go quietly,' the princess told the BBC in 1995, 'and it didn't; and then when we were married they said it would go quietly and it didn't; and then it started to focus very much on me, and I seemed to be on the front of a newspaper every single day...' As isolating as this newfound fame was, Diana knew her new role was a huge privilege, and the princess took it very seriously. Her outfits for official public engagements – always thronging with fans – were meticulously planned, each something of a coded message. Her off-duty looks were just as exciting, from effortless ensembles to marvellously mannish suiting and everything in between.

Diana's own style evolution is a story told in millions of photographs, news reports, and paparazzi shots. From her early days as 'shy Di' to the ultimate 1980s power dresser, and finally the confident, considered personal style that emerged after the break-up of her marriage – known to some as her 'revenge look'. Eventually, Diana used her celebrity to draw attention towards her humanitarian work, turning what had once been an intrusive, uncontrollable force into something that might just power a new role for her, as a patron of charities, an advocate and friend of the forgotten, and as a loving mum to her two sons, William and Harry.

Much has been made of Diana's lifelong difficulties with the palace; she laid them bare in a feted BBC *Panorama* interview in 1995 with Martin Bashir. As her marriage collapsed, her place in the royal family was thrown into question. And yet, just before her death – that fatal car crash in Paris in August 1997 – Diana had reached a new milestone in life. She had just auctioned 79 dresses from her past life as a royal wife and possible future queen of England; symbolically shedding one persona in order to create another. She may have lost the battle, but she had won the war, and seemed stronger, serene, and had

THE YOUNG PRINCESS WAS THE ULTIMATE 1980S SUPER-SLOANE

———•———

a newfound optimism; she had fallen in love. An interview with *Vanity Fair* in July that year, with its memorable Mario Testino photo shoot, was entitled 'Diana Reborn'. She passed away just weeks later.

'I'd like to be a queen of people's hearts,' Diana once said, imagining a new future for herself, a legacy to leave behind. This book is a celebration of the Princess of Wales, her love of fashion, of life, and her everlasting influence on culture, celebrity, and style.

'I LIKE TO BE
A FREE SPIRIT.
SOME DON'T
LIKE THAT,
BUT THAT'S THE
WAY I AM.'

———————•———————

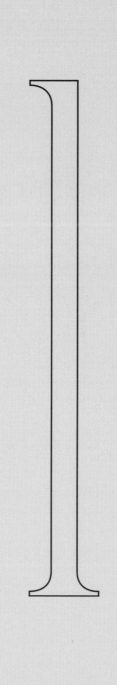

SHY
DI

Meet Lady Diana Spencer, the young, relatively unknown British noble the press dubbed 'shy Di', all doe-eyes peeping out from behind feathered bangs, her face prone to flushes, thrust suddenly into the spotlight. Her sense of style was sweetly naïve, quaint, and – at times – wonderfully uncool.

———————◦◦◦———————

'AT THE AGE OF 19,
YOU ALWAYS THINK
YOU'RE PREPARED FOR
EVERYTHING, AND YOU
THINK YOU HAVE THE
KNOWLEDGE OF WHAT'S
COMING AHEAD.'

At the age of 13, Diana had already met her first love: a hairy little beast known as Soufflé. The tiny Shetland pony lived at her mother's home in Scotland, and Diana was besotted. Diana lived with her father, Edward John Spencer, the 8th Earl Spencer, but in the summer holidays, the young tomboy was able to live out the season in the Scottish wilds with her mother, Frances Shand Kydd. Diana gave out young Jodie Foster vibes with denim jeans, pale blue-grey V-neck wool sweater, polo shirt and her own thick, dark blonde mane.

In July 1979, Diana's mother bought her an apartment at Coleherne Court in Earl's Court as an 18th birthday present. Like many of us, as a teenager, she found it hard to find her place in the world, or a career that would stick. But she loved children and, at 19, she found herself as a nanny for the Robertson's, an American family living in London, and worked as a nursery teacher's assistant at a posh school in Pimlico. With rumours of a burgeoning relationship with the bachelor Prince Charles, the young Diana began to find herself the object of attention of the British press. She was papped wearing this outfit – rich brown car coat, slim pants, flat loafers and devil-may-care neck scarf – as she trotted through Mayfair's Eaton Square, perfectly accessorised with a small bemused child in a pushchair.

In late 1980, the press heard a delicious royal rumour: bachelor king-to-be Prince Charles had a new girlfriend – but who was she? Ahead of the prince and Lady Diana Spencer's official engagement announcement in February 1981, newspapers fought to be the first to reveal just who this mystery girl was. Arthur Edwards, then royal photographer of British tabloid newspaper the *Sun*, was trusted with this impossible task. The *Sun* had heard Diana worked in a children's nursery in London, and so Edwards trawled the city trying to find her. After visiting a number of nurseries – and being turned away at each one – he finally stumbled onto Diana's place of work. Perhaps naïvely, she agreed to have her photo taken and Edwards took her to nearby St George's Square in Pimlico.

Diana wore a simple tonal outfit: lilac heart-print patterned skirt, pastel shirt, and purple wool V-neck vest, but halfway through the impromptu shoot, the sun came out, shining through her skirt, offering Edwards a glimpse of her legs. The image appeared on the front page of the *Sun* (which featured daily topless female models on its infamous 'Page 3' until 2015) alongside the headline 'Charlie's Girl'. Reminiscent of the upskirting scandals of contemporary times, Diana was horrified, and the image became one of the first syndicated images of the princess-to-be.

THE BLACK SHEEP

This super-cute sweater in pillar box red with a flock of white sheep (and one black one) became the archetypal 80s knit when Diana wore it to a polo match in 1983. Styled up with a crisp white Peter Pan collar, black ribbon bow, and gradient aviators, the princess' hair at that point was peak-Lady Di: feathered and full. Die-hard Di fans love this sweater; some might say she was seen as the black sheep of the royals, for a time. It's now part of the permanent collection at the V&A Museum in London.

This Peruvian-style sweater with cute llama motif has become something of a fan favourite in recent years with DIY knit patterns and vintage versions selling online. Diana wore it for an outdoors photo call at Balmoral with Charles just before their wedding, teaming it with high-waisted khaki corduroy trousers and cream silk turtleneck, thick red socks and that iconic accessory of the posh countryside set: green wellies.

STEPHEN JONES

All hail the punk king of hats. One of the original Blitz Kids – the flamboyant New Romantic students who hung out at London's celebrated Blitz nightclub in the late 70s and early 80s – Stephen Jones made hats for nightlife stars. As a young clubber, he rubbed shoulder pads with the likes of Boy George, Jean Paul Gaultier, Isabella Blow and Grayson Perry.

After the onetime punk's successful collection for Fiorucci in 1979, Blitz owner Steve Strange helped bank roll the young Stephen Jones's brand. His art school cool and celeb clientele allowed Jones to pivot his customer base towards the cream of London society, and he soon counted Princess Diana as one of his loyal fans. 'She knew [wearing a hat] was part of being royal,' said Jones in 2017, '…she understood… that it was part of the responsibility – to be identifiable. It was a symbol of royalty…'

Diana loved other high-end milliners, too, from Philip Somerville to Graham Smith of Kangol, John Boyd and Frederick Fox. To create bespoke millinery for Diana, each designer had to follow royal etiquette, meaning their designs must never have wide brims that might hide the face from onlookers – and they must be firmly fixed in place. Jones' handmade berets were perfect, created for a young Diana in her 20s, rendered in slouchy rich velvets or suede, giving each hat a slightly relaxed, youthful look. He embroidered each one with her initials and the Prince of Wales feathers.

As Diana's personal style evolved, and her place in the royal family was renegotiated, it was hats off for her favourite milliners as she started to break with protocol and wear less headpieces, but Jones has always had a special place in the hearts of the royal family. Kate Middleton is a fan, and Meghan Markle wore a white Stephen Jones beret at the Commonwealth Service in March, 2018, a pleasing nod to her late mother-in-law, perhaps.

Diana wore this delightful Victor Edelstein hot pink gown to the opera in Italy in 1985. It featured double spaghetti straps and bows, and had the added sparkle of the 'Cambridge Lover's Knot Tiara', created for Queen Mary in 1914 (and now worn by Kate Middleton). The House of Garrard diamond and pearl topper was inspired by a headpiece owned by Queen Mary's grandmother Princess Augusta of Hesse, with Mary reusing her own 'Ladies of England Tiara' to create it.

Fresh from a sitting for her first official portrait by Bryan Organ, commissioned by the National Portrait Gallery (unveiled just before her wedding, weeks later), Diana stepped out with Charles for a night at the Royal Academy of Arts in London. It was June 23, 1981, and a rare unofficial event; a small party of sorts, hosted by then academy director Sir Hugh Casson. The dark sparkle of her simple, blueberry shift sequin dress with metallic spaghetti straps and matching wafty bolero, held in hand, delighted her fans. It was the perfect shade, to bring out her eyes, and she accessorised the look with sapphire and diamond jewellery, and a rather shy, classic Diana look.

They weren't the only ones who enjoyed a royal soirée that night. While Diana and Charles partied with Sir Hugh, three German medical students 'mistook' the royal gardens of Buckingham Palace for Hyde Park, sneaking through a gap in the wall. They camped out in the grounds overnight and breakfasted on beer before they were discovered and moved on by armed palace guards the following morning.

Three months after the royal wedding, Diana stepped out for an official engagement in a pale blue and white diaphanous Bellville Sassoon dress. It was the opening of the Splendours of the Gonzaga exhibition at the Victoria and Albert Museum in London on November 4, 1981, celebrating the art and treasures of the ancient Northern Italian dynasty. At the beginning of the 17th century, Vincenzo Gonzaga, the fourth Duke of Mantua, gathered together an A-team of the finest painters and baroque musicians, dedicating his time to artistic pleasure. Diana's dress was perfectly romantic, dreamy and sheer with an off-the-shoulder tier, fastened with pale blue ribbon. Splendid, indeed.

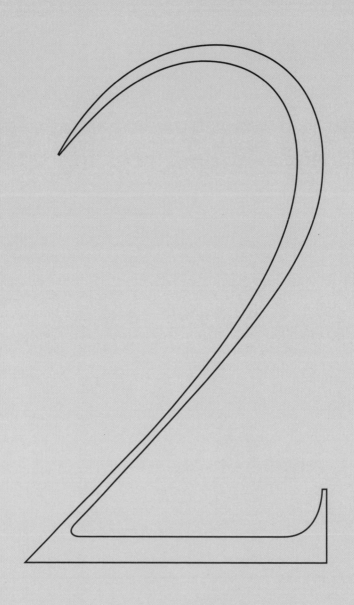

A ROYAL
LOVE STORY

As Diana navigated her new celebrity, she jumped headfirst into royal duties, and discovered the art of regal power dressing. Already making almost daily headline news, her wedding to Prince Charles in 1981 was watched by 750 million people, and her wedding dress became an overnight icon.

'THE DAY I WALKED
DOWN THE AISLE AT
ST PAUL'S CATHEDRAL,
I FELT THAT MY
PERSONALITY WAS TAKEN
AWAY FROM ME, AND
I WAS TAKEN OVER BY
THE ROYAL MACHINE.'

———————— • ————————

On February 24, 1981, Diana wore a two piece in the most royal of royal blues, styled with a pussy bow blouse and glossy black clutch. After weeks of rumour and gossip, the press was finally summoned to Buckingham Palace for the first appearance of a newly engaged couple, Prince Charles and Lady Diana Spencer, and Di's blue outfit set off her engagement ring of sapphires and diamonds. The couple wandered the palace grounds as cameras clicked, and an endearingly romantic and impossibly cute TV interview followed with blushes from Diana and bluster from Charles. The young couple had everything ahead of them.

ELIZABETH AND DAVID EMANUEL

British design duo Elizabeth and David Emanuel, then husband and wife, are the undisputed creators of one of the world's most famous and influential fashion designs: Diana's wedding dress. The couturiers, graduates of the Royal College of Art, were a favourite of Diana Spencer, but their commission to make the princess-to-be's marital robes was not without controversy.

At first, the pair seemed to be something of a leftfield choice. When they got the call that would change their lives forever, they had only graduated a year previously, yet every well-known designer in the world wanted to make Di's wedding dress. Not only were they given just three months to produce it, working right up to the eleventh hour, they had the added pressure of keeping the design a secret, and even had to hire security to ensure it wasn't leaked.

On July 29, 1981, their design was finally revealed: it had all the pomp of a Disney fairy tale wedding, but also seemed to mesh perfectly with the centuries' old tradition of an English royal dynasty. Diana emerged from a horse-drawn carriage billowing in oodles of ivory silk, taffeta, and antique lace, hand-embellished with 10,000 pearls and sequins, and an impossibly long, 7.5 metre (25 foot) train that flowed down the cathedral steps like buttermilk. While 750 million people tuned in to watch live on TV, crowds in London were euphoric. It was a triumph, setting a new craze in wedding design, and within weeks, church aisles and registry offices were awash Diana-style puffed sleeves, full skirts, and gauzy vintage veils. Weddings would never be the same again.

Canadian designer Donald Campbell created many of Diana's most memorable dresses, starting with this floral wrap dress she wore leaving Eastleigh Airport in Hampshire, UK, heading off on her Mediterranean honeymoon with Charles. Toronto-born Campbell was a master of 'modern classic' dressing, offering a demi-couture service from his London boutique, but Diana was the first to debut a piece from his ready-to-wear collection, worn with a pearl choker and a smile.

On November 5, 1981, the palace announced Diana and Charles were expecting their first child. Two hours later, arriving at a private lunch with the Lord Mayor of London at the Guildhall, the crowds had descended, eager to see – and congratulate – the new mother-to-be. Diana wore an outfit debuted a week before on a trip to the windswept Welsh Isle of Anglesey, an artsy-looking russet brown full-length coat with oversized embroidered running stitch detailing, fringing, and topped and tailed with matching blue hat and heels. The Guildhall luncheon – attended by hundreds – heard a heartfelt speech of congratulations by the mayor, with Diana blushing furiously at the frenzied attention.

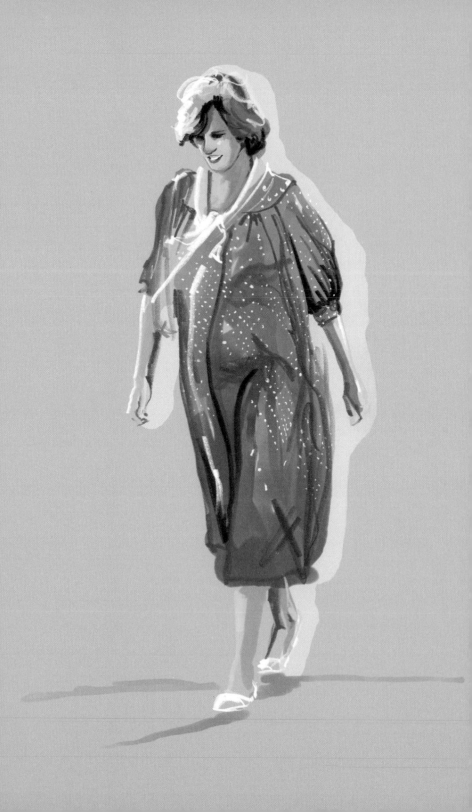

Much has been made of Diana's maternity style, with outfits ranging from traditional, ultra-femme maternity wear, voluminous and simply cut, to more formal ensemble for official events. Her go-to was the oversized shirtdress in soft tones, like this green polka dot mat-dress with pussy bow detailing, symbolising the slightly stuffy royal style she eventually grew out of.

The inimitable Jenny Kee is one of Australia's most celebrated designers, cultural influencers and bon vivants. The onetime model from Bondi would entertain stars like David Bowie at her Flamingo Park boutique in Sydney, founded with creative co-conspirator Linda Jackson, and spent time with the in-crowd in London in the Swinging 60s. Today, Kee is known for a trippy, psychedelic style and gorgeous silk scarves. She is very much the designer's designer; Karl Lagerfeld used her prints for his debut collection for Chanel, and contemporary brand Romance Was Born paid homage to Kee with its Paris show in 2018.

In 1981, Kim Wran, the daughter of New South Wales Premier Neville Wran, sent newlyweds Charles and Diana a pair of koala and kangaroo motif jumpers designed by Kee. A year later, Diana, pregnant with William, was photographed wearing the koala jumper at a polo match. 'It was in every newspaper, magazine around the world,' Kee told the *South China Morning Post* in 2019. When Kee was finally introduced to the princess in Australia in 1983, she 'called her Di – a terrible faux pas,' recalls Kee in her 2006 autobiography *A Big Life*. 'I apologised profusely, but she was all warmth and grace. "No, please call me Di," she said, and went on to explain she'd put my name on the guest list herself because she loved my jumpers.'

On August 4, 1982, Diana and Charles posed for official photographs at the christening of their first son, Prince William Arthur Philip Louis of Wales, in the music room at Buckingham Palace. It was also the 82nd birthday of the Queen Mother and all the royals were in attendance – with the palace machine running the show (giving Diana very little say in proceedings). With a nation hoping to guess the baby's name, George was the favourite (bookmakers offered odds of 1000–1 on the name Elvis), but William it was. Diana wore a pink floral frock with matching pink hat, and William wore a delightful dress himself: the Honiton white lace gown, worn by many royals at their christening, first commissioned by Queen Victoria in 1842.

Diana's party dresses are legendary. Although some might seem somewhat frozen in the style of the time, others have gone on to influence contemporary designers. This Bruce Oldfield concoction, worn to a fashion week party in 1982 – a few months after Diana gave birth to Prince William – is one such frock. With its daring one-shoulder cut and impossibly voluminous ruffles, Oldfield created this piece in one of Di's signature colours: royal blue. It featured a 3D ring print, low 80s waist and a slightly bonkers pompom detail at the mid-section. It may have all the trappings of 1980s high glamour, but fashion fans believe it may have influenced the Gucci Spring 2017 runway show; one showstopping regal-looking gown offered Diana vibes with its one-shouldered, ruffled royal blue realness.

On June 11, 1984, pregnant with Prince Harry, Diana wore an eye-popping Catherine Walker creation to a glamourous red-carpet film premier (Spielberg's *Indiana Jones and the Temple of Doom*) with Charles at the Empire Cinema in London's Leicester Square. With her hair styled like a 1930s starlet, Diana's pale blue satin frock shimmered under the flashbulbs. Walker gave the double-breasted piece tuxedo detailing, shoulder pads that allowed the dress to drape beautifully, and a swathe of satin cascaded down into a loose bow over Diana's baby bump.

July 18, 1986, and Diana's next trick was to take her sons on a mini pony-trek on the grounds of Highgrove House in Gloucestershire (now the family residence of the Prince of Wales and the Duchess of Cornwall) for a photo shoot. Diana wore one of her staple off-duty pieces, the white shirt. Loved by Diana devotees and London's Sloane Rangers, the white shirt soon became stuck in the collective fashion consciousness. In the 1980s, Diana accessorised it with a string of pearls, or a simple sweater thrown over the shoulders. And it's hard to say which was cuter: the young Prince William cavorting on a Shetland pony, or Diana's lifechanging floral pants, but it's a close call.

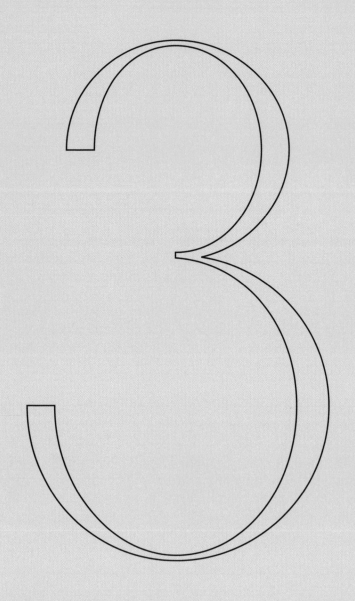

80s
HIGHLIGHTS

As Diana's style evolved,
she started working with a wider
pool of designers, and her new look
helped set the decade's luxe style.
From daytime outfits by Jasper
Conran, to gorgeous red-carpet
ensembles from Bruce Oldfield,
and her beloved friend, Gianni
Versace, Diana became a symbol
of the 80s glamour.

'ONLY
DO WHAT
YOUR HEART
TELLS YOU.'

———•———

When Kate Middleton, Duchess of Cambridge, stepped out in a bright red houndstooth coat on a public engagement in Stockholm, Sweden in 2018, fans of Princess Diana raised a collective eyebrow. It seemed an homage, in part, to Diana's iconic oversized houndstooth suit she wore to Princess Eugenie's christening in 1990. Kate's coat was designed by Catherine Walker (one of Diana's favourite designers); Diana's was Moschino, but both looked as if they had been cut from the same cloth.

Both Prince William and Prince Harry's wives, Kate and Meghan, have referenced their late mother-in-law's style, in ways both subtle and knowing, to creating visual parallels – with a contemporary spin.

Diana wore this red houndstooth cropped blazer with a white and black scarf roped through the collar. The outfit had a matching black houndstooth pencil skirt, and Diana wore the suit again in 1991 on a trip to Canada, and also in March 1992 on a visit to the National Hospital for Neurology and Neurosurgery in London, in her role as patron.

BRUCE OLDFIELD

Couturier Bruce Oldfield's upbringing was anything but royal. Born in 1950, Oldfield grew up in County Durham, UK with his seamstress foster mother, and later, at a Dr Barnardo's care home for children in need. But, with hard work, talent, and a little mischief, Oldfield graduated from Central Saint Martins College of Art, and went on to design collections for Henri Bendel department store in New York. On his return to London, and with a cool new NYC-edge, Oldfield began to make a name for himself as a celebrity dresser. It was Charlotte Rampling who helped Oldfield hit the big time. She asked him to design the costumes for her film *The Purple Taxi* (1977) and, within a year, Oldfield was able to establish his own fashion line.

His showstopping gowns are thought to have helped refashion Diana's style, evolving it from her go-to cardigans and Laura Ashley skirts to a glamourous, impeccably dressed A-lister, sashaying down the red carpet at film premiers. In 1985, the princess wore Oldfield's legendary metallic silver evening gown, pleated and backless, on the red carpet at the *A View to a Kill* premier in London. The event, attended by the film's stars Roger Moore and Grace Jones, was a celeb-studded affair, but the real star was Diana, glittering and ethereal in Oldfield's Grecian-style gown.

Diana loved all-plaid looks – a style note Kate Middleton and Meghan Markle have been keen to keep up with. There are hundreds of images of the princess in plaid outfits, from subtle pastel tartans to this more daring two-piece she wore at Aberdeen Harbour aboard HMY *Britannia*, Scotland in August 1986. The double-breasted jacket with puffball sleeves had a matching fishtail skirt, cinched in with an oversized black belt. Diana styled it with a fuchsia pussy bow blouse, a matching shocking pink clutch and gravity-defying hair.

Diana loved Emanuel, the British fashion house founded
by Elizabeth and David Emanuel, who created her wedding
dress. In April 1985, she wore one of Emanuel's most eye-
catching couture creations on a trip to Venice. A formal
daytime look, the voluminous teal plaid coat had oversized
lapels and impossibly huge shoulder pads, stretching out
wide than the brim of her already rather wide matching hat.
Diana styled the look with a simple ivory lace-edged slip and
a string of pearls. Years later, the piece was rediscovered,
purchased at auction by Historic Royal Palaces, and added
to the 'Diana: Her Fashion Story' exhibition at Kensington
Palace in 2017. Both Kate Middleton and Meghan Markle
seem to have drawn inspiration from the coat, wearing
toned-down contemporary versions of Diana's fashion-
forward ensemble.

CATHERINE WALKER

'Mummy, that's too awful to sell,' said Prince William, apparently, when his mother added her infamous 'Elvis dress' to a charity auction inventory. Created by Catherine Walker, the French-born Brit couturier beloved by Diana in the early 1980s, the two-piece – nicknamed the Elvis dress for its popped collar and thousands of pearls – helped make £3 million for AIDS charities.

Of course, the dress wasn't officially inspired by the King himself, but rather an official trip to Hong Kong in 1989. The softly sparkling co-ord was made up of 20,000 hand embroidered pearls, and – like many of Di's Catherine Walker commissions – the outfit was made specifically with the traditions of the destination in mind (the Chinese are considered the inventors of the cultured pearl), but with a British princess edge. Although many fashion critics deplored what they saw as over-the-top pageantry, the clean-cut column dress and bolero expertly straddle the divide between pared-back minimalism and regal, devil-may-care splendour. Di wore the dress again to the British Fashion Awards, seemingly as a subtle tsk to her critics.

Walker herself passed away in 2010, but her husband, Said Cyrus, keeps Catherine's brand as client-focused and luxurious as ever, and counts Kate Middleton as a fan. The curator of the Christie's show, Meredith Etherington-Smith, made sure the dress went to a good home: memorabilia-makers The Franklin Mint snapped it up and eventually released a Princess Diana doll wearing the ensemble, before donating the dress to the Victoria & Albert Museum in London.

The princess wore this delightfully upbeat candy stripe outfit to Royal Ascot. The horse racing event has been a firm fixture on the royal social calendar since 1711 when Queen Anne devised what would become an annual three-heat horse race. By 1752 it was the social event of the year, and by the early 19th Century, Royal Ascot's strict dress code came into effect, powered by the Prince Regent's infamous style-loving friend Beau Brummel. Little has changed, and today – as in Princess Diana's time – Royal Ascot is something of a formal fashion parade. Each year, the focus is Ladies Day where the great and good turn up in their most upscale ensemble; with hats (not fascinators) a must.

Diana wore this diaphanous red striped pussy-bow blouse to Ascot in 1981, with long red vest, matching skirt with leather cord belt and matching red hat. It was one of the princess' more outlandish looks but, she loved it, wearing it again on a royal tour of Australia in March 1983.

MILITARY PRECISION

In April 1987, Diana visited the Sandhurst Military Academy for its annual passing out parade, wearing a military-style skirt suit by Catherine Walker with gold brocade and a white hat by Graham Smith at Kangol. Both William and Harry attended the prestigious academy in Surrey, UK alongside royalty from around the world.

Diana knew all too well the rules of royal etiquette: the length of a hemline, the angle of a hat, the right occasion to wear gloves, pearls, or some ancient precious gem and how to hold up a clutch bag across one's cleavage as you emerged from a car. She excelled at following the rules, but only up to a point, and eventually she found her own path to tread. She called her critics – the fusty establishment pundits and tabloid commentators – the 'grey men'; what better way to get one up on them by dressing as one herself? Diana's personal style saw her borrow from men's fashion design, from her double-breasted blazers, tuxedos and car coats, to this delightfully masculine look with gold embellished blazer, necktie, gold buckle belt and brown suede Chelsea boots.

With varsity prints, Disney motifs, and such, Diana's sweatshirt addiction knew no bounds, but some were more audacious than others. In recent years, a personal snap of the princess has started to do the rounds, with Diana wearing a sweater of pure 1980s indulgence. The photo, a family pose with a very young William and Harry on a swing, sees the princess in a hot pink slogan sweater with 'I'm a Luxury...' emblazoned across the front, and – rumour has it – the back slogan '...few can afford.'

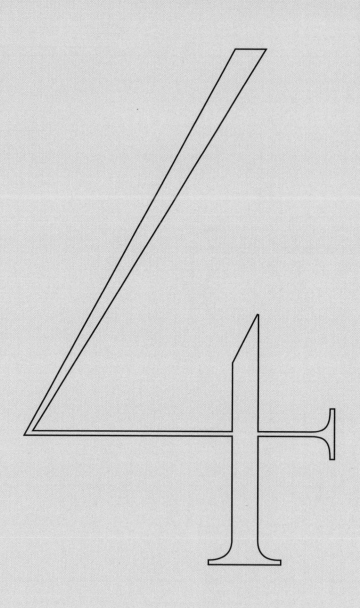

ROYAL TOURS & HOLIDAYS

Some of the most enduring images of the princess' style document her tours of the Commonwealth and beyond, from dancing with John Travolta at the White House, to wandering alone at the world's greatest monument to love, the Taj Mahal; to presenting an award to a group of wet and wild lifesavers in her beloved Australia.

———◦◦◦———

'PEOPLE THINK
THAT AT THE END
OF THE DAY A
MAN IS THE ONLY
ANSWER. ACTUALLY,
A FULFILLING JOB
IS BETTER FOR ME.'

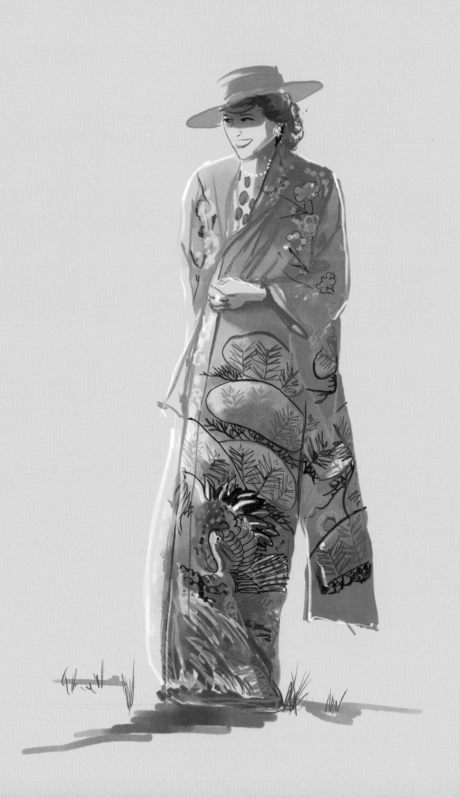

On a five-day official tour of Japan in 1986, Diana took part in a Japanese tea ceremony with Charles at Kyoto's celebrated Nijō Castle, which dates back to 1679. It was glorious weather and the princess was shown two delicate kimonos which had been brought out into the sunshine for her to see. One was ancient and priceless, and – in a break of royal protocol – she was invited to try on the other, a £40,000 pale peach kimono. It was placed tentatively over her carefully chosen ensemble (a white dress with red polka dots) – and the crowd went wild.

VICTOR EDELSTEIN

At Ronald Reagan's state dinner at the White House in 1985, Diana chose a design by London-born Victor Edelstein, the onetime Biba designer and couturier who had already created many of the princess' most memorable dresses. The rich, midnight-blue velvet Edelstein gown was a floor-length, off-the-shoulder number with ruched detail and looked enchanting in full swing. Luckily, John Travolta – encouraged by Nancy Reagan – was there to lend a hand.

Travolta's dance card has always been full of the best names in showbiz, from Olivia Newton-John in *Grease* and Karen Lynn Gorney in *Saturday Night Fever* to Uma Thurman in *Pulp Fiction*, but the White House dinner was perhaps his first rumba with royalty. Some claim the photo was a press opportunity (although, it seems both Di and Travolta were unaware) and the sight of a Hollywood royalty and a real princess dancing to the *Saturday Night Fever* soundtrack certainly made the headlines.

Edelstein worked for Christian Dior in London before opening his own design studio in 1977. From 1982, he focused purely on couture becoming London's go-to for deliciously glamourous evening and event wear, and Diana was one of a select group of Victor-fans who commissioned five or six dresses each season. Wearing a Brit couture star was the perfect choice for a White House dinner, but it was Diana's clever styling – using John Travolta as the perfect accessory – that helped the gown hit the front page, becoming one of the princess' most memorable looks.

PRINCESS OF THE
BUDGIE SMUGGLERS

In 1988, on a Royal tour of Australia and New Zealand with Prince Charles, Diana agreed to present a prize to the winning team of lifesavers at the Central Coast Surf Carnival at Terrigal Beach, in New South Wales. It was one of five visits Diana made to the country over 15 years; she loved Australia and after what was to be her final visit in 1996, it was thought she might actually move there. Australians were fascinated with the royal family, and Diana herself was widely adored.

That day at Terrigal she toured the seafront with Charles, waving at the crowds from a sleek, black open-top Jeep, before posing for one of the most enduring and iconic images of the princess in Australia. As she presented the prize, she was photographed surrounded by Terrigal's finest – Central Coast Council lifesavers and volunteers – clad in their tiniest swim briefs, known affectionately as 'budgie smugglers'. Dressed in a loose-fitting white summer dress with yellow floral print, she looked slightly shy – and yet utterly delighted, laughing at the situation.

Ah, the Canadian Tuxedo. Diana, known for her brave fashion choices, was undeniably a fan of the double denim look. On a trip with her sons to the exclusive ski resort in Lech, in the heart of the Austrian Vorarlberg, the princess wore mid-tone stonewashed denim Mom jeans (with a rather comfy-looking high waist) and matching denim Western shirt, accessorised with a pair of moon boots. Diana's love of Lech underlined the resort's exclusive image, and past visitors include the Dutch and Jordanian royal families, and Monaco's Princess Caroline. It was in Lech in April 1997 that Prince Harry – then aged 12 – learned to ski, and he has been a regular visitor to the Alps ever since.

Diana always looked happy and relaxed with she visited Australia. She wore this pink polka dress with high gathered neckline by Donald Campbell during a visit to Perth, styled with a matching John Boyd hat, where she attended an open-air children's display at Perth Hockey Stadium in Bentley with Charles. Decades later, Kate Middleton wore a similar dress by Oscar de la Renta to an official engagement in Southern Ireland, but with all the 1980s panache of her late mother-in-law.

The Royals love Swiss ski resort Klosters, especially Charles (there's even a cable car named after him, the 'Prince of Wales'). On a trip with Diana in 1986, she wore a dark pink Head ski suit, accessorised with a matching tonal braided headband in crimson, pink and white. After Diana's death, Charles continued to take William and Harry to Klosters for what became an annual father-and-son trip while the two princes were growing up. The three even took a trip to the upscale ski resort before Charles's wedding to the Duchess of Cornwall in 2005.

GIANNI VERSACE

In the 1990s, fabled Italian design powerhouse Gianni Versace was perhaps the most beloved and successful fashion designer in the world. With his friend Princess Diana, the pair created a number of legendary fashion moments, not least the electric silk gown she debuted at the Victor Chang Cardiac Research Institute Royal Ball in Sydney. In 1996, Princess Diana embarked on an official tour of Australia, and the Versace Atelier one-shouldered dress was a true showstopper. Gianni really understood what suited Diana; one-shouldered gowns always looked great on her statuesque frame, but the colour and relative simplicity of the gown made it an iconic look.

Versace also dressed Diana for a *Harper's Bazaar UK* shoot in 1991 with photographer Patrick Demarchelier, and the images appeared on the cover in 1997, just after her death. The sleeveless Versace Atelier column dress – apparently the first Gianni made for the princess – is rendered in pale blue silk with gold studs, and bejewelled with glass beads in aquamarine, sky blue and white, and reached almost $200,000 at auction in 2015.

Versace and Diana passed away in 1997, both in shocking circumstances. In *Vanity Fair*, published just two weeks before his own death, Versace said of the princess: 'I had a fitting with her last week… and she is so serene… It is a moment in her life, I think, when she's found herself – the way she wants to live.' Diana attended Gianni's funeral on July 22, 1997 and passed away herself less than a month later.

On Charles and Di's 1985 tour of Italy, crowds gathered at the Duomo in Florence to catch a glimpse of the royal couple. Diana chose a stark, brilliant white suit by Jasper Conran, accessorised with a black men's bowtie. Diana spent much of the day with male clergy, in their black ceremonial robes, and her contrasting ensemble – the cutting edge of contemporary British fashion – seemed divinely inspired.

JACQUES AZAGURY

When Moroccan couturier Jacques Azagury first met Diana, he was overwhelmed and simply stared, open-mouthed. 'I was dumbstruck,' he recalls. In 1987, the onetime club kid had just launched his New Romantics collection when Anna Harvey, *Vogue*'s deputy editor, introduced him to the young princess. His shyness – and glamourous designs – charmed Diana and she asked to visit his atelier shortly after. Azagury went on to create some of Diana's most memorable looks, and he remained one of her favourite designers until her death in 1997.

Schooled in East London, Azagury studied at the London College of Fashion and Central Saint Martins before setting up his own slick Knightsbridge space after graduating. Diana's visits were hugely exciting for the designer and his team. 'She was always interested in what everyone had to say,' Azagury told journalist Sandy Rashty in 2019. 'She would ask about my life, she would talk to the girls in the atelier and tell them she liked their nail varnish.'

Kensington Palace was less than a 10-minute drive away from the Knightsbridge store, and Azagury visited for fittings, meeting Diana's young sons: 'They were her big love.'

Of all the dresses Azagury created for Diana, a bright red mid-length dress she wore on a tour of Italy in 1995 is one of his most memorable designs. 'The princess always looked amazing in red,' says Azagury, and his discretely sparkling two-piece gown, impeccably cut, was debuted at the Venice Biennale. Arriving at the Peggy Guggenheim Collection by boat, Diana met her host, art patron David Tang, on the museum's dock, ahead of a celeb-studded reception. It was golden hour; the sun was setting, and Diana and her red dress were illuminated against the ancient Venetian facades, the canal glittering behind her.

In July 1997, Diana and her boys were on holiday in St Tropez in the South of France. The press speculated the princess was visiting Castle St Thérèse, Dodi Al-Fayed's 30-bedroom villa. It was a sun-filled beach and boat holiday, and Diana wore an animal print one-piece swimsuit as she spent time with her sons, Princes William and Harry. It would be the last holiday the three would spend together.

The Taj Mahal, the sublime ivory-white marble mausoleum built in Agra, India in the 1600s, is known to the world as a testament to love. Built by Mughal emperor Shah Jahan in honour of his late wife, Mumtaz Mahal, the complex of stunning buildings plays host to more than eight million tourists each year, forming the backdrop to marriage proposals, stolen kisses and lovers' stage-managed selfies.

By the time of Diana and Charles's visit in 1992, things had soured between the prince and princess. He met business leaders, made speeches and helped launch a new charity. She sat, alone, on a bench in front of the Taj Mahal. Diana wore a colour-block outfit in rich tones, a simple gold hoop neck piece, and – amidst rumours of an unhappy marriage – photographs of the event made headline news around the world. BBC diplomatic and royal correspondent Peter Hunt said in 2016 that 'Diana… who understood the power of imagery – said it had been a very healing experience. Asked what she meant, the princess replied: "Work it out for yourself."' Charles and Diana announced their separation within the next 12 months, and 20 years later, her son and daughter-in-law, William and Kate, recreated the iconic image – prince and duchess, together.

CASUAL ELEGANCE

She may have been a 'queen in people's hearts', but Diana was also the undisputed queen of street style. Her thrown-together outfits had a casual elegance; they seemed effortless, contemporary – and delightfully oddball. From baggy sweatshirts and cowboy boots to marvellously mannish suiting, the princess was utterly ahead of her time.

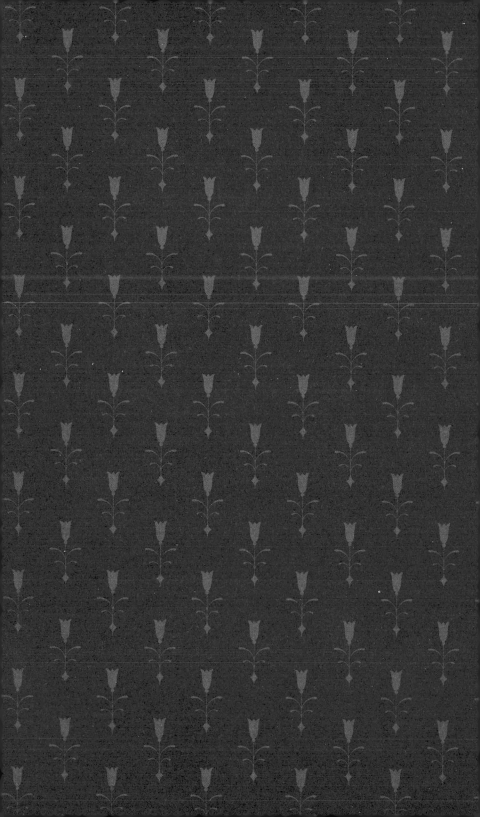

'I DON'T GO
BY THE RULE
BOOK... I LEAD
FROM THE
HEART, NOT
THE HEAD.'

————— • —————

This winter look, with its clever contrast of volume, is timeless. Diana made a dash through the snow in the mid-90s in these skinny black jeans, brown suede Chelsea boots and huge (and impossibly cosy-looking) down jacket in a bright red. Topped off with a vintage-looking blue mesh baseball cap (with the insignia of the Royal Canadian Mounted Police) and a cool pair of shades. It's an ensemble that wouldn't look out of place right now in the checkout-line at Trader Joe's; Diana's style is just as relevant today as it was then.

A LITTLE BIT COUNTRY, A LITTLE BIT ROCK 'N' ROLL

Much has been said about the 'It' dresses Diana wore to special events, creating iconic fashion moments with the world's top designers, couturiers and fashion houses. But her style was just as powerful off-duty as it was sashaying along the red carpet. This gloriously mis-matched outfit with loose, high-waist stonewash Mom jeans, placement print charity sweatshirt (Diana was a patron of the British Lung Foundation), dark sports jacket, cap and leather cowboy boots was recreated in 2019 for a *Paris Vogue* photo shoot, with Hailey Bieber stepping in to Diana's shoes. Bieber later commented that Diana was 'amazingly beautiful and iconically stylish'.

THE HIV/AIDS
ADVOCATE

In 1987, Diana attended the opening of one of London's first purpose-built HIV/AIDS ward at Middlesex hospital in London. Stigma, fear and misinformation meant that people infected could be shunned by friends and family; images of the princess shaking the hand of a man with AIDS became a powerful example of compassion.

Advocating for those living with the illness which seemed to have affected gay men worst of all, Diana became interested in the work of HIV centre London Lighthouse, then the largest centre of its type in Europe. Onetime volunteer David Hodge remembers a surprise appearance from the princess in the 1990s. The visit caught him somewhat unawares, meaning he had forgotten to put away the lewd-shaped club flyer he was using as a bookmark. 'She must have known the affect she had on people and how nervous I had suddenly become,' he told *Gay Star News* in 2017, 'so she smiled very sweetly and then said: "I love your bookmark". My response was to look down and let out a half shriek as I realised what she was looking at! At this, she started to laugh her head off!'

Hodge recalls how Diana helped take away the 'dirty' connotations around HIV and AIDS and legitimise it as a genuine illness that affects everyone, not just gay men.

Millionaire entrepreneur Richard Branson gifted Diana
this Virgin Atlantic sweatshirt and she used it wisely.
Her trainer, Jenni Rivett, recalls how Diana would wear
it to almost every gym session, foiling the paparazzi
who couldn't sell photos of her in the same outfit days
in a row.

Whatever Diana wore was culturally powerful. Her outfits could kickstart fashion trends, designers she loved would gain a new, loyal fanbase, and hairstylists around the world would keep their clients freshly clipped with the latest Diana 'do'. The princess knew this and harnessed her star-power for charity work. In particular, images of her infamous 1997 walk across a minefield in full body armour and visor helped bring the invidious problem of landmines to the world's attention.

Diana had worked with the British Red Cross for several years before the charity helped facilitate her trip to Angola. There, in Huambo province, she encountered The Halo Trust which had worked as clearing landmines since 1994. She met landmine survivors, many of them children (Prince William and Prince Harry, back at home, were only 14 and 12 years old at the time) and was escorted by students and mine-clearance experts through an active minefield. The photos were snapped up across international media and gave an unforgettable portrait of the princess, making the humanitarian landmine crisis headline news.

Di loved a sweatshirt. Her fondness for the gym saw her appear in many athleisure outfits; it was a clear indication of how her position as a royal, and a celebrity, had evolved. She was recasting herself as a stronger, more resilient woman, a mother with muscle. Ever since, the oversized varsity style sweatshirt has been a touchstone of celebs and stylists; its timeless appeal has seen contemporary stars and influencers channel the late princess' off-duty style.

Is there anything more Instagrammable than a khaki military jumpsuit and contrasting pink Converse sneakers? Diana wore this *en pointe* ensemble on a visit to see the 13th/18th Royal Hussars display on Salisbury Plain, UK. She was kitted out in simple, army-issue khaki overalls – and looked delighted about it.

The royals are snow-sport addicts, known for whooshing through the white stuff at the world's most exclusive ski resorts. With the Alps a short flight from the UK, the Duke and Duchess of Cambridge love French resort Courchevel, first visiting in 2016. Verbier in Switzerland is another hotspot – it's where Princess Eugenie and her husband Jack Brooksbank met in 2010. The most well-known royal ski destination is Klosters and, in February 1986, Charles and Diana spent a few days there with Sarah, Duchess of York and Prince Andrew. Diana took to the slopes in mirrored sunglasses and a rather 1980s ski suit and looked as though she loved every minute of it.

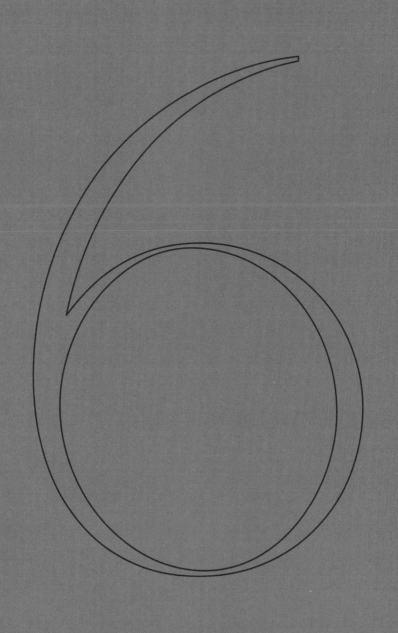

LADY IN
RED

The princess could (and would) wear almost any shade, and many of her most memorable fashion moments involved bold tones and primary colours. Much of a royal woman's job – particularly for official engagements – was to stand out from the crowd and red was one of Diana's favourites. The princess shone in scarlet, crimson, claret and everything in between: bow down to the original 'Lady in Red'.

'EVERYONE
NEEDS TO
BE VALUED.
EVERYONE HAS
THE POTENTIAL
TO GIVE
SOMETHING
BACK.'

———•———

Jasper Conran was one of the princess' favourite designers, and this scarlet two-piece wool suit was one of her best-loved Conran custom-made designs. She debuted it in November 1984 at the official naming ceremony of the cruise liner *Royal Princess* (named in her honour). Diana loved red so Conran chose a rich scarlet hue to help the young royal stand out in the crowd.

On March 4, 1982, Diana and Charles attended an event at London's Barbican Centre, the city's modernist marvel of arts venues, piazzas, water features and apartments. The previous night, the Queen had opened the Centre's new arts venue, and its first event was 'The Night of Knights: Royal Gala' presented by David Frost (interviewer of President Nixon), in aid of the Order of St John and the Prince's Trust. Pregnant with Prince William, Diana wore a floor-length, high-waisted dress in a rich red satin, with square neck edged in white lace, three-quarter sleeves with ruffles and a silver clutch with matching ballet flats.

On a two-day trip to Norway in February 1984, Diana wore a Jan van Velden gown to see the London City Ballet perform at the Oslo Konserthus. It was her first solo trip as a royal, and – as patron of the dance company – Diana was star guest for its performance of *Carmen* on February 11. She wore a luxurious black velvet cloak that fell open to reveal a bright cherry red floor-length van Velden piece, with sheer appliqué long sleeved top over matching slip, and floor-length skirt, diamond drop earrings and an informal pearl choker.

In October 1988, Diana attended a state reception in Melbourne, and – squished into a crowd of male photographers – it was camerawoman Jayne Fincher who took one of the most iconic shots of the princess in Australia. 'From the start, we got along very well,' explained Jayne in the book, *Diana: Portrait of a Princess (1998)*, '...we became friendly since I was the only woman among the crowd of cameramen who regularly covered the world's most famous family. I often felt that when she gazed into my camera lens, her look was different from the ones she directed at my male colleagues. Her expression was more relaxed and vulnerable with me.' That night, Diana dressed in flame-red and gold, in a bright slash-neck dress with voluminous '80s shoulder pads, pencil skirt with slits and an open, V-shaped back. Her earrings were a leaf design, set in gold, and the look was confident, subtle and powerful.

This laid-back ensemble – one of Diana's polished post-workout outfits – shows how her personal style evolved. By July 1996, the princess' new-found confidence shone, just like this bright red wool overcoat, thrown effortlessly over her workout gear, worn with white socks and sneaks and a post-aerobics-class glow.

For a dinner at the British Embassy in Paris in November 1988, Diana wore Catherine Walker, choosing to show off the British designer's fashion prowess in the world's chicest city. The princess was on an official visit to France, and the gown was a sublime satin one-shoulder affair with a scarlet rose repeat-print, with ruching for added dimension. There was something pleasingly audacious about the princess wearing a British designer to a French event, but the dress – daring and unique – was a hit.

July 20, 1989, and Diana stepped out for a state banquet at Claridge's hotel in London in full sparkling regalia. The floor-length Bruce Oldfield dress – jewel-bright ruby red with subtle silver windowpane check – had '80s ruching, long corset waist, with draped capped sleeves and flowing skirt. Diana was there to meet members of the UAE and wore diamonds, a tiara and accessorised with matching red shoes and clutch.

A child's first day at school is always a nerve-wracking affair: dropping your little monster off at the school gates with break-time snacks, juice box and a teary eye. But imagine the added pressure of a gaggle of photographers desperate to capture every moment. In September 1989, Diana arrived at Wetherby School in London's Notting Hill neighbourhood with William and Harry for Harry's first day. The boys – beyond excited – wore their grey and red school uniforms, and Diana chose a complimentary red outfit, with appliqué red sweater, long pleated skirt and red shoes.

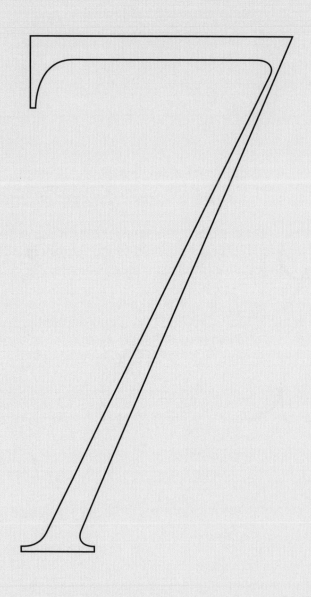

REVENGE
LOOKS

Die-hard Di fans all know and
love the 'Revenge Dress', designer
Christina Stambolian's LBD the
princess wore to the Serpentine
Gallery in 1994. After the slow-
motion break-up of her marriage,
Diana's style evolved once more;
she was powerful, confident,
and just a little bit racy.

'FROM NOW ON,
I AM GOING TO OWN
MYSELF AND BE TRUE
TO MYSELF.

I NO LONGER WANT TO
LIVE SOMEONE ELSE'S
IDEA OF WHAT AND
WHO I SHOULD BE.
I AM GOING TO BE ME.'

CHRISTINA STAMBOLIAN

Ah, the 'Revenge Dress': perhaps the most sizzling sartorial decision the princess ever made. In 1994, a TV documentary aired in the UK in which Prince Charles revealed his affair with Camilla Parker-Bowles. That same night, the media – frothing over with excitement to see Di's reaction – camped out at *Vanity Fair*'s star-studded Serpentine Gallery summer party in London, desperate to pap the princess' reaction. Perhaps they imagined a nervous, teary woman on the verge, but what they saw that evening was something quite, quite different.

Three years previously, Greek-born designer Christina Stambolian delivered the princess a rather racy drop-shoulder LBD with plunging back, in form-fitting pure silk but, at the time, it was just too slinky and sexy for royal protocol. It was yanked out of the closet as a last-minute replacement for the Serpentine party (Di's planned Valentino outfit had been leaked to the press), and Diana stepped out in front of the cameras in Stambolian's masterpiece. Nicknamed the 'Revenge Dress', Di wore it with simple black heels, sheer hosiery, and accessorised it with a pearl choker (the one she wore to a White House dinner where she danced with John Travolta), blood red nails and a newfound, seemingly unshakable confidence. It was daring, powerful, and completely off-brand, and the media – realising they had been deliciously wrong-stepped – went wild. Anna Harvey, Di's former stylist, said she wanted to 'look like a million dollars' that night, and by all accounts, she did just that.

In August 1997, days before her death, Diana found herself back in Saint-Tropez, France, with her boyfriend Dodi Al-Fayed. The princess wore this neon one-piece with matching sarong as she danced in the sunshine on a yacht.

Diana adored Chanel and had a special relationship with the feted French fashion house. For her son William's confirmation, she wore a classic Chanel bouclé suit from Karl Lagerfeld's Spring/Summer Couture line in 1997. That March, she debuted the pale blue bouclé wool suit with fringed lapels and matching above the knee skirt, with matching pillbox hat, Chanel bag and heels. In fact, she loved it so much, she wore it again a month later ata British Lung Foundation event.

DIOR

To Paris, 1995, as Bernadette Chirac, the First Lady of France, gifts Diana a Dior handbag for the opening of a Cézanne exhibition at the Grand Palais. The princess loves it; immediately ordering more from the famous French fashion house, and the accessory becomes an overnight icon, earning itself a place in fashion history.

The small black leather bag has signature Dior quilting (a nod to the Napolean III chairs set out for Christian Dior fashion shows), and a twinkle of lucky metallic charms. By 1996, after becoming associated with the princess, the bag known as '*Chouchou*' was officially re-named, and the Lady Dior bag became the world's most wanted accessory.

However, legend has it that this historical moment almost didn't happen. The bag, designed by Gianfranco Ferré, had been made for the very first time the night before the Cezanné opening, with the house's craftspeople racing to meet a near-impossible deadline. Then, as now, each Lady Dior bag is made by hand. Made of butter-soft lambskin, 140 pieces are cut, assembled, and sewn together with Dior 'cannage' top stitching and four golden Dior letters. Comparable only to the Hermès Birkin, Fendi's Baguette and Chanel's 2.55, the Lady Dior remains one of the world's most desired 'It' bags, and we have Diana (and Dior's legendary all-nighter) to thank for it.

Diana's cheetah print one-piece swimwear with matching kaftan was perfect for a really wild holiday in the British Virgin Islands in 1990.

This blush pink tailored suit, designed by Gianni Versace for a visit to the troops, is one of Diana's most iconic looks. It's hard not to see Versace's clever nod to Jackie O; the ensemble was seemingly inspired by the pink Chanel suit worn by Jackie Kennedy on the day President John F. Kennedy was assassinated. The suit itself was a masterstroke: impeccably cut and achieving a balance between vintage-edged formality and a youthful, upbeat, femme look. Invoking the style of Jackie O, a woman well-known for her approach to style and diplomatic power, underlined Diana's own place in politics. Her pillbox hat was to keep her love of millinery firmly fixed in place.

SALVATORE FERRAGAMO

In her days as princess-to-be, Diana would follow tradition, diligently wearing the formal day bags from royal Warrant holder Launer, beloved by Princess Margaret and The Queen Mother. It was a rather old-fashioned expectation of the young royal who had become interested in fashion, so later she would have her dressmakers and couturiers make her handbags. Only they could create something with a precise colour match, a style trick in-keeping with royal tradition, but with just enough flair to excite. But, by the 1990s, Diana broke royal protocol, investing in glossy European couture brands, with Italian fashion house Salvatore Ferragamo a favourite.

There was one Ferragamo bag Diana loved, and she collected approximately 20 of them. The calfskin accessories with their famous gold-hooped 'Gancio' clasps and glittering chain straps soon became an 'It' bag. They are now retrospectively known as the Lady D.

Salvatore Ferragamo, Italy's most celebrated shoe designer, has been a fashion icon since the 1930s, and – before Diana – had already designed for political and Hollywood 'royalty', making shoes for Eva Peron and Marilyn Monroe, respectively. Salvatore passed away in 1960, but his family still own the brand, designing shoes and accessories in his innovative spirit. The Lady D bag remains one of the brand's most admired styles.

THE DRAG KING
PRINCESS

There is an urban legend about Princess Diana that – if true – could be one of the most fantastic, delicious and surprising stories ever told about her. Rumour has it, one mischievous night in 1988, a chance conversation with her friend, Queen frontman Freddie Mercury, ended with the pair boozing with friends in a notorious London gay bar with Di under the radar in a camo jacket, leather fetish cap, aviators and a fake moustache.

The bar in question is the Royal Vauxhall Tavern (RVT), the first building in the UK awarded with special listed status because of its cultural significance to the gay community. 'Freddie told her we were going to the [Royal] Vauxhall Tavern – a rather notorious gay bar in London,' British celeb Cleo Rocos told the RVT's *Tales of the Tavern*. 'Diana said that she had never heard of it and she'd like to come too. Now this was not a good idea... But it was clear that Diana was in full mischief mode... She just wanted the thrill of going in, undetected. They had the modest aim of getting to the RVT, ordering a drink and bundling Diana into a cab without her being recognised – and they achieved it.' Rocos remembers Diana thought she would be recognised any minute, but no one seemed to notice the Princess of Wales in full drag, and she blended into the background. 'She loved it,' says Rocos.

Diana's beachwear and bikinis feels as relevant today
as they did in the 1990s. Statement glasses, high-waisted
one-pieces, loose-fitting oversized tees – and this two-
piece bikini with gathered bra top and matching sarong
are just as Instagrammable as contemporary luxury
swim brands.

In July 1997, just weeks before her death, the princess did something extraordinary. Seeking to mark her transition from royal underling to woman in charge of her own destiny, she auctioned off 79 of the dresses she wore as the wife of the future King of England. The symbolism of the sale at London's Christie's auction house was clear, and the money raised went to five of Diana's favourite charities. Two years previously, she had given her infamous BBC interview, emerging as a woman on the verge. Now, relaxed and effervescent in a South London studio trying on frocks with celebrity fashion photographer Mario Testino, she was something else entirely.

Ahead of the sale, Testino shot a series of portraits of the princess as she listened to Italian pop diva Dalida and tried on some of the dresses up for sale, thereby creating some of Diana's most iconic images for *Vanity Fair* magazine. In the accompanying article, Cathy Horyn feverishly wrote of the princess' latest incarnation in the cover feature Diana Reborn: 'Diana's appeal as a postmodern icon resides solely in her ability to renew and transform herself – and, by racing just slightly ahead of our imagination, to hold us in constant thrall.'

ACKNOWLEDGEMENTS

The author would like to thank: artist and illustrator Fernando Monroy; art director Evi O and her team; publisher, editor and royal style enthusiast, Kate Pollard; Kajal Mistry, Maggie Davis, Rachel Johnson, Sue Jones, Isabel Davis, Nella Van Veenendaal and Lauren Hawthorn.

ABOUT THE AUTHOR

Dan Jones is based in London, writing about style and fashion, queer culture and history, and his first love, booze. His favourite Diana style era is the 1980s: anything with big shoulder pads, big hair and a truckload of diamonds.

ABOUT THE ILLUSTRATOR

Fernando Monroy is an artist based in Mexico City, who uses pop culture as his inspiration.

@fmonroyr

Published in 2020 by Hardie Grant Books,
an imprint of Hardie Grant Publishing

Hardie Grant Books (London)
5th & 6th Floors
52–54 Southwark Street
London SE1 1UN

Hardie Grant Books (Melbourne)
Building 1, 658 Church Street
Richmond, Victoria 3121

hardiegrantbooks.com

British Library Cataloguing-in-Publication Data. A catalogue
record for this book is available from the British Library.

Diana: Style Icon
ISBN: 978-1-78488-381-2

10 9 8 7 6 5 4 3 2 1

Publishing Director: Kate Pollard
Design and Art Direction: Evi O. Studio | Nicole Ho & Susan Le
Illustrations: Fernando Monroy

Colour reproduction by p2d
Printed and bound in China by Leo Paper Products Ltd.